Jira Handbook

The Step by Step Jira Manual with Illustrations for Beginners

By

Jonjo Penney

Table of Contents

Chapter 1: Getting Started with Jira Data Center

Understanding the Jira platform

J ira began as a well-liked project management and tracking application for software development teams. Jira has expanded to address the needs and difficulties of its users as the IT sector has evolved. Jira now offers extra features and capabilities beyond issue tracking. It has evolved from being a single application to a platform with multiple applications and solutions that can run on top of it.

The Jira family of products comprises various offerings from Atlassian, the company that created Jira. They consist of the following:

- **Jira Software:** This product is mostly concerned with software development. Project teams can manage software development projects utilizing classic waterfall and agile approaches like Scrum and Kanban.

- **Jira Work Management:** This product is made for teams who don't build software, like those in marketing, operations, and law. It is ideal for all-around task management.

- **Jira Service Management:** A product for service desk staff is this. It is made to run Jira as a support ticketing system, with a streamlined user interface for end users and an emphasis on Service-Level Agreement (SLA) goals and customer satisfaction.

Jira Software and Service Desk build specialized features on top of the Jira platform, which at its core offers many of its basic functionalities for various products, including user interface modification, workflows, and email notifications.

Of course, Jira's status as a platform makes it possible for other outside developers to create solutions for it. Jira offers many more functionality thanks to the enormous, vibrant ecosystem of partner products and services provided by Atlassian. In a later chapter of this book, we shall examine some of these options.

Jira Software will be the main topic of this book, but we'll also go over all the features that all the applications have in common and how each application might use them. For this reason, unless an explicit distinction is required, the name "Jira" will be used to refer solely to Jira Software.

After learning more about the Jira platform and its different products, it's time to examine the newest Jira family member.

Introducing Jira Data Center

Scalability is one of the greatest issues users frequently have with Jira Server. An organization's Jira deployment may frequently encounter performance concerns, such as slower response times, once it reaches thousands of concurrent users and hundreds of thousands of issues. Customers frequently had to archive and export old projects to another Jira instance or divide their one huge instance into numerous smaller instances, even though each new major release would improve performance.

Some businesses can overcome this issue by switching to the Jira Cloud service. But not everyone can use the public cloud because of security concerns, legal restrictions, or because they prefer to run Jira on their private cloud. Jira Data Center can help with this.

The new Atlassian service, Jira Data Center, which replaces the outdated Jira Server, intends to address issues frequently encountered by businesses that want a performant, scalable, highly available, and secure Jira deployment.

You can keep hosting Jira yourself with Jira Data Center and enjoy the abovementioned advantages. Many new features include support for Security Assertion Markup Language (SAML), advanced planning roadmaps, and enhanced administrative functionality.

System requirements

We need to consider the hardware and software needed for Jira and how you want your deployment to go before we can implement Jira Data Center.

Jira can be used in one of two ways:

- **Standalone:** This deployment is identical to the traditional Jira Server, in which a single Jira instance serves all of your users. This is the simpler choice and uses fewer system resources. This is the best choice if you're just starting.

- **Cluster:** This deployment allows you to run several Jira instances (also known as nodes) that serve your users. This is your solution if you require scalability, high availability, and other cluster-specific capabilities.

You can always start with the standalone option if you need clarification about which to choose and transition to a cluster when you require all the features and advantages of a clustered deployment.

Hardware requirements

Jira will function smoothly on any server with a 1.5 GHz processor and 1 GB to 2 GB of RAM for test purposes, with only a few users. As your Jira usage increases, a typical server will have a quad-core 2 GHz+ CPU, 4 GB of Memory, and at least 10 GB of hard disk space specifically allocated for the Jira program.

You should run Jira on a separate dedicated server for production deployment, as you would with most applications. When selecting how much funding to give Jira, you should consider various elements, including how Jira will expand and scale. You should take into account the following when determining your hardware requirements:

- The number of users who are actively using the system at any given time, particularly during peak usage

- The number of projects, problems, and remarks in the system

- The number of configuration elements, such as workflows and custom fields.

It can be challenging to estimate these numbers at times. For comparison, a server with a 2.0 quad-core CPU and 4 GB of RAM will be adequate for most situations with 200 active users. You must dedicate at least 8 GB of Memory to Jira if you experience thousands of active users (JVM). The benefits of simply increasing system resources (vertical scaling) start to fade once a Jira instance has more than a million issues and many active users. In these circumstances, it is frequently preferable to consider adopting Jira's Data Center version. It provides higher scalability by enabling you to cluster many instances together (horizontal scaling) and supports high availability.

Jira officially supports only x86 hardware and its 64-bit versions. Jira can use more memory while running on a 64-bit system than on a 32-bit system, which is a maximum of 4 GB. You should utilize a 64-bit OS to deploy a sizable instance.

Regarding software, Jira has three main requirements: a supported operating system, a Java environment, and a database to house all its data. We will go over each of these needs and your options for installing and using Jira in the following sections.

Software requirements

The decision of which operating system to run Jira on depends on knowledge, comfort, and, in most cases, the infrastructure and requirements of the current organization. Jira supports the majority of the major operating systems.

Windows and Linux are supported operating systems by Atlassian. Although there is a Jira distribution for macOS, it is primarily used for testing. Amazon Web Services (AWS) and Microsoft Azure are also supported with quick-start templates.

Installation package options

There are many deployment options available with Jira Data Center. Where you want to deploy Jira is the first decision you need to make. Atlassian offers quick-start templates if you wish to install Jira to AWS or Azure so you can get started right away.

You can use the installation packages if you want to manage how Jira is deployed or if you want to deploy it to your hardware or other cloud providers. There are two types of installation packages for Jira:

- **Executable installer:** This installer takes you step-by-step through the installation procedure using a wizard-driven interface. To save you time, it even includes a Java installer.

11

- **TAR.GZ or ZIP archive:** The archive package is comparable to the executable installer, but it lacks the installation wizard, bundles Java, and configures Jira to run as a service. A few manual post-installation tasks, including setting up Jira as a service, will also be required. You do, however, gain the advantage of understanding how things work.

Although we will utilize the installer package for our exercise, we will also go over the post-installation procedures, so you know the different configuration options available.

Installing and configuring Jira

Jira will first be set up as a standalone deployment. The installation will be done on a Windows platform, and PostgreSQL will power the database. Go to the vendor guidance on installing the necessary software for your platform if you intend to use a different platform or database.

Installing Jira

These are two crucial locations we must specify before installing Jira:

- **JIRA_INSTALL:** The Jira program will be installed in the directory.

- **JIRA_HOME:** This is where some of Jira's crucial configuration and data files will be kept.

There are two steps for installation in general:

- Installing and downloading the Jira program

- Completing the Jira setup wizard

Obtaining and installing Jira

The Atlassian website will automatically identify your operating system, which will then recommend an installation package for you to download. Choose the appropriate operating system package if you plan to install Jira on a different operating system than your current one.

As we previously stated, there is a Windows installer package and a self-extracting archive package for Windows. We will use the installer package for this practice (Windows 64-bit Installer):

1. To launch the installation wizard, double-click the downloaded software file and select the Next option.

2. Click the Next icon after selecting the Custom Install (recommended for advanced users) choice. Jira can be installed anywhere we choose by using the custom installation, which also offers a variety of configuration choices, as seen in the screenshot below.

3. Choose the installation location for Jira. This location will be used for JIRA INSTALL. To proceed, click the Next option.

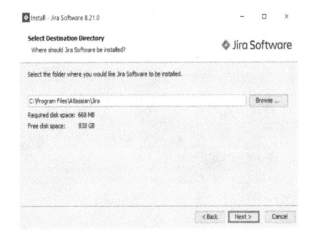

4. Choose the location for Jira's data to files, including documents and log files. The JIRA HOME subfolder will be created here. To proceed, click the Next option.

5. Choose the location where you want to add shortcuts to the Start menu, then select the Next button to proceed.

6. In the Configure TCP Ports step, we must choose the port Jira will use to wait for incoming connections. Jira will operate by default on port 8080. Select the Set custom value for HTTP and Control ports option and enter the port numbers you want to use if another application has taken 8080 or if you want Jira to operate on a different port, such as port 80. To proceed, click the Next option.

7. Choose whether you want Jira to function as an application. If you enable this option, Jira can start automatically with the server; see the Starting and stopping Jira section for more information. Jira will be installed as a system service if you enable this option.

8. The last stage is to review all the options for installation and then click Install to begin the installation:

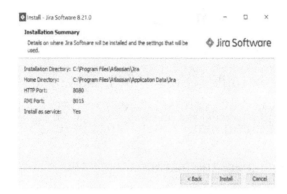

9. After the installation is finished, select the choice to launch Jira Software in a browser and click Finish. By doing this, you can end the installation wizard and enter Jira through your web browser. As Jira launches for the first time, this might take a while to open.

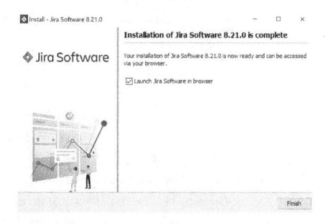

The Jira setup wizard

The Jira setup wizard should appear in your browser window if you selected the Launch Jira Software in Browser option during the installation wizard's final stage. If not, open your browser and navigate to http://localhost:port number> where port number> denotes the port you gave Jira in Step 6 of the installation procedure.

Jira's user-friendly setup tool will guide you through finishing your setup. You can set the primary language, database connections, and many other things here.

The following are the methods to do this:

1. We must choose how Jira will be set up in the wizard's first stage. We will choose the I'll put it up myself option because we are installing Jira in a production environment.

2. We must choose the database we want to use in the second stage. Here is where Jira's PostgreSQL database configuration is made. Jira will use its integrated in-memory H2 database if you choose the Built-In choice, which is useful for testing. Choose the My Own Database if you want to use a legitimate database.

Set up application properties

Existing data? You can import your data from another installed or hosted Jira server instead of completing this setup process.

Application Title   Jira
                     The name of this installation.

Mode   ⦿ Private
          Only administrators can create new users.
        Public
          Anyone can sign up to create issues.

Base URL   http://localhost:8080
            The base URL for this installation of Jira.
            All links created will be prefixed by this URL.

Next

3. In the third stage, you must provide fundamental information about this Jira instance. When you've finished with the required fields, select Next to proceed to the next phase of the wizard:

Set up application properties

Existing data? You can import your data from another installed or hosted Jira server instead of completing this setup process.

Application Title   Jira
                     The name of this installation.

Mode   ⦿ Private
          Only administrators can create new users.
        Public
          Anyone can sign up to create issues.

Base URL   http://localhost:8080
            The base URL for this installation of Jira.
            All links created will be prefixed by this URL.

Next

4. A Jira license key must be provided at this stage. The textbox labeled "Your License Key" is where you should enter the license key that Atlassian provided. By selecting the link to "generate a Jira trial license," you can create an evaluation license if you don't already have one. The trial license gives you access to everything Jira offers for one month. You can still view your data even

after the evaluation time has ended, but you can no longer create new issues.

5. You must now set up Jira's master account. You must store the account information safely and remember the passcode. You won't be able to recover the password because Jira only saves the password's hashed value, not the password itself. Enter the administrator account information, then select Next.

6. You must then configure your email address information. Jira will issue email notifications using the data set up here. One of Jira's most effective features and a key method of user communication, notifications, are

very strong. If you don't have your email server information on hand, you can bypass this step for the time being by choosing the Later option and hitting Finish.

Congratulations! Your Jira build-up is complete. The administrator account you set up in Step 5 should now be loaded on the welcome screen, and you should be logged in as that user. On the site's first page, you can change settings like your preferred language and upload a profile photo. To create the account, adhere to the displayed instructions. When you're done, you'll see a screen like the one below, where you can either make a sample project, start a new project, or import data from another source.

Clustering

Our Jira instance is currently operating in standalone mode, which means it is fulfilling all requests independently and has yet to be activated for clustering. The following are some of the key advantages of using a cluster to operate Jira:

- **Improved performance at scale:** Jira can better fulfill concurrent user requests by operating in a cluster with numerous nodes, which improves response times and customer satisfaction.

- **High availability and failover:** As long as several nodes operate in a cluster, your users won't experience any downtime even if one of the nodes goes unavailable for whatever reason.

- **Zero-downtime upgrade:** Jira upgrades typically need downtime because of the nature of the operation. You can upgrade each node in a Jira cluster one at a time so that the other nodes in the cluster can keep providing service to your users.

The following must be done to set up Jira to operate in a cluster:

- Make a shared file home directory accessible to both nodes.

- Our present Jira instance needs to have cluster configuration added.

- Install a second Jira instance to serve as the cluster's second node. Technically, a cluster can consist of just one node, but we'll include another node for this exercise to allow you to observe the cluster in operation.

- Add and configure a load balancer to distribute incoming traffic to both nodes.

Preparing for clustering

The preparation of the necessary hardware is the first step in enabling clustering. You will have the following elements for a Jira cluster:

- **Load balancer:** Any load balancer that supports session affinity (sticky sessions), such as Apache and nginx, can be used as a load balancer.

- **Jira instance node:** The cluster's individual Jira instances will be located on this Jira instance node.

- **Database:** You use the same database for your standalone deployment. Note that the in-memory H2 database won't function in a cluster because every Jira node will use the same database.

- **Shared file drive:** Each Jira node must have access to the shared home directory of the Jira cluster to function properly.

For a two-node cluster, you will require a minimum of three servers and a shared network drive because each of the components listed above should ideally be running on its server. The advantages of having a cluster are diminished when running multiple Jira nodes on the same server, so you should only do this for testing purposes.

The following needs to be taken into consideration when setting up servers for Jira nodes:

- The same data center or geographic area houses all of the node servers.

- Your hardware and software requirements, such as memory, operating system, and Java version, are the same.

- Jira is running on the same version on all nodes. The nodes have been set up to share a time zone.

Creating JIRA_SHARED_HOME

Creating a new directory for the cluster to store its data files is the first step. This folder will be referred to as JIRA SHARED HOME. Any Jira nodes may be able to read from and write to this network disk. The JIRA HOME directory of your standalone Jira instance should be copied over to the new shared directory, along with the following directories:

- data

- plugins

- logos

- import

- export

- caches

Enabling clustering

The next step is to make your first Jira node cluster-capable. To accomplish this, a new cluster.properties file is added to the JIRA HOME directory on the local machine.

1. Close the solitary Jira instance.

2. New file cluster.properties should be made.

3. The files with the following lines:

   # This ID must be unique across the cluster

   jira.node.id = node1

   # The location of the shared home directory for all Jira nodes

   jira.shared.home   = /location/to/the/shared/jira_cluster_home

   # The following lines are needed if you want to run multiple nodes on the same server

ehcache.listener.hostName=localhost

ehcache.listener.port=40001

ehcache.object.port = 40021

4. Start jira.

Adding new nodes to the cluster

Follow these steps to add a new node to the cluster:

1. Transfer the JIRA HOME directory from the old node server's Jira instance to the new one.

2. On the new server, install a fresh instance of Jira.

3. Change the jira.node.id value in the cluster.properties files.

4. Fill out the load balancer with the new node.

5. Launch the fresh Jira node.

As described in the section Updating Jira's port number and context path, if you are running the second node on the same server, you will also need to change the port numbers for ehcache.listener.port and ehcache.object.port in the cluster.properties file and the port numbers in the server.xml file.

And with that, your two-node Jira cluster ought to be operational. Currently, both nodes should be listed in

Administration | System | Clustering when you log into Jira, with the node presently serving you highlighted in bold.

Zero-downtime upgrade

As previously discussed, you may do a rolling upgrade with zero downtime while running Jira in a cluster. You can upgrade every node in the cluster one at a time with a zero-downtime upgrade. There won't be any downtime for your users because other nodes in the cluster will keep providing service while a node is being upgraded.

The steps involved in performing a rolling update are as follows:

1. Upgrade Jira by switching it on. As a result, the Jira cluster can run nodes with various versions concurrently.

2. Each node in the cluster is upgraded separately.

3. Once all nodes have undergone an upgrade, complete the upgrade.

Jira will be switched to Upgrade mode to begin with:

1. Log in as an administrator in Jira.

2. Go to Jira upgrades under Administration | Apps.

3. Set Jira into upgrade mode.

You can upgrade a cluster node by shutting it down after Jira has been put in Upgrade mode. Once a node has undergone an upgrade, you can restart it and carry out this procedure on the cluster's other nodes.

You must complete the upgrade by performing the following actions after you have upgraded each node in the cluster:

- Navigating to Jira upgrades under Administration | Apps.

- Tap on Finalize upgrade.

The upgrading process for your cluster will be finished once you click Finalize Upgrade. You can upgrade your entire cluster without affecting your users' access by doing a rolling upgrade like this.

Chapter 2: Using Jira for Business Projects

Jira was developed primarily as a bug-tracking tool to assist software development teams in tracking and managing the issues and difficulties in their projects. People started utilizing Jira for additional things as the product developed. Others use it as a customer service site, while some use it as a general-purpose job management system. Jira can be utilized inventively, including monitoring financial portfolio performance.

Understanding projects and project types

While using Jira, one of the most crucial ideas is a project. A project can stand in for anything, from a team or department within a company to a real software project or an IT helpdesk. A project can be considered a collection of work items known as issues. As users develop and deal with concerns, it aids in giving context. A support team will work within a helpdesk project, while a software development team will deal with issues in a project that has been formed for the product they are working on.

Project types aid in defining the project's goal and offer users a customized user experience and set of features. For instance, a project for service management will have features like service-level agreements (SLAs), but a project for software development will support Scrum or Kanban.

To aid you in getting started quickly, each project type includes one or more templates with various predetermined options.

Business projects

Jira offers a variety of project kinds, as we've already seen, based on the features you have access to. The business project type comes pre-configured, and its templates are primarily designed to make it simple for users to set tasks and track and report on their progress.

Project, task, and Process management are the initial three templates, each with predefined setups like processes and fields. Depending on your needs, you can utilize them as-is or further alter them. Other project kinds exist, including those in service management and software development.

Jira permissions

Before getting into projects, having a basic understanding of permission is important. We will now briefly discuss project administration, creation, and viewing permissions.

There are many levels of permission in Jira.

- **Global permission:** Manage Jira setup, add and remove projects

- **Project permission:** Permission to view and manage specific projects

- **Issue permission:** Look through specific issues

Project creation and deletion will be permitted for Jira administrator global authority users. Getting Started with Jira Data Center will be able to create new projects because users in the Jira administrator group, by default, have this permission. We shall refer to this user as a Jira administrator and any other users who possess this privilege.

Users that have the project's Administer Projects permission can manage the configuration settings for each given project. Users with this permission can access the Project settings interface for a specific project. This enables them to modify the project's setups and specifications. The Jira administrator will, by default, have access to this.

A user must have Browse Projects permission for a given project to browse its contents. This indicates that the user will have access to the project's Project Browser interface. The Jira administrator will, by default, have access to this. After going over the fundamentals of Jira permissions.

Creating projects

Using the Create project menu option from the Projects drop-down menu in the top navigation bar is the simplest way to start a new project. By doing this, the Create project dialog will appear. You can only choose this option if you have this privilege.

Choose the template you want to use from the New Project dialog's Business header, then click Next. Jira will show the predefined configurations for your chosen template on the following page. As we've chosen the Project management template in our example, Jira has given us two different issue kinds and a process with just three simple stages. To proceed, click the Choose button.

Project user interfaces

In Jira, there are two unique project interfaces. The project's reports, statistics, and agile boards are usefully explained in the initial interface, which is made for regular users. This interface will be referred to as the Project Browser interface.

We will refer to the second interface as the Project Settings interface because it is intended for project administrators to manage project configuration settings, including permissions and workflows.

The Project Browser interface will be the first you encounter after creating a project. Before looking at the Project Settings interface, we will begin by looking at this interface.

Project Browser

Depending on the kind of project you create, the Project Browser will change. For commercial endeavors, it is fairly easy. The left-hand panel has a few tabs that are accessible.

The Summary tab

You can view the project you're working on on a single page using the Summary tab. For business projects, it offers an activity view, which will show the most recent project actions, and a statistics view, which gives you numerous helpful breakdowns of the project's problems.

The Issues tab

The project's open issues are listed on the Issues tab by default. You can search for problems using several additional predefined filters that are included. You can choose a specific topic from this list to learn more about it.

The Versions and Components tab

All versions and components for this project are listed on the Components and Versions tabs, respectively. These two views are available only if the project contains versions and/or components.

Project settings

Project administrators can control the settings and configurations of their projects through the Project settings interface. For instance, you can modify the project's key and name, decide which issue kinds will be accessible, and maintain a list of its constituent parts. People with Administer Projects permission for a specific project can only use this interface.

Observe these steps to access the Project settings interface:

1. For the project you want to manage, visit the Project Browser interface.

2. At the bottom left, choose Project settings. You only have the required permits if you can see this option.

Using the Project settings interface, you can perform the major actions listed below:

- The project's name, description, avatar, and type should be updated.

- Control the problem types, fields, and screens users view when working on the project.

34

- Set the project's workflows to your specifications.

- Control notification and permission settings

- Control the list of components and versions that are offered.

Importing data into Jira

Jira allows you to import data from additional sources, such as other issue tracking systems, and notifies you if the data can be exported in a supported format, like CSV or JSON. The interface of each importer is driven by a wizard that leads you through a sequence of steps. There are a few changes, but these steps are similar overall. While importing data into Jira, four steps are often involved:

1. Choose your source data, such as a CSV file.

2. Choose a destination project where the imported issues will go. This could be a new initiative conceived on the spot or an existing project.

3. Map the fields in the source (such as a CSV file) to the fields in Jira.

4. Map Jira field values to source field values. This is typically necessary for select-based fields, such as the priority or list fields. For fields such as text and numeric fields, this is not necessary.

Importing data through CSV

The CSV importer with Jira enables you to import data in the comma-separated value (CSV) format. This tool is helpful as most systems can export data in this format. This program can also turn an Excel spreadsheet into a CSV file.

- Ensure your data is formatted correctly before attempting to import it into Jira through a CSV file. The following list of things you should check before importing your data:

- Ensure you have all the values for the issue in a single row because each row must be imported as a single issue.

- There should be a field in Jira for each column. Either a system field or a custom field may be used for this.

- At the very least, you must fill out the mandatory fields, such as the issue summary.

- The format of every date or date-time value must be uniform.

- Ensure the username values for any columns mapped to user fields, such as assignee, are accurate.

- Check the spelling of the values if a column is to be mapped to a selection-based field, such as a choice list or a checkbox.

Once your CSV file has been formatted, import it into Jira by following these instructions:

1. From the Projects drop-down menu, choose Import External Project.

2. Choose CSV by clicking on it. The import wizard will launch as a result.

3. You must choose the CSV file containing the data you wish to import by clicking the Choose File button.

4. When the source file has been chosen, expand the Advanced section to choose the CSV file's encoding and delimiter. There is also the option to Use an existing configuration file, which we will discuss in more detail in the following section.

5. To continue, click the Next button.

6. The project you want to import your data must be chosen. To start a new project immediately, choose the Create New option.

7. Make careful to include the format used in the Date format box if your CSV file contains date-related information.

8. To continue, click the Next button.

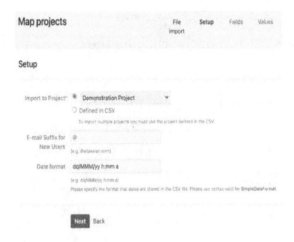

9. The CSV fields (columns) must then be mapped to the fields in Jira. It's optional to map some fields. Simply choose not to map the CSV field to a Jira field if you do not want to import data from a specific column.

10. You must choose the Map field value checkbox for fields like select list fields that need to have their data manually mapped. This will enable you to correctly import the data by mapping the CSV field value to the Jira field value. If these values are not manually mapped, they will be copied to their current state. There will be automatic creation of new options for fields like choose lists.

11. To continue, click the Next button.

12. The last step is mapping the CSV field value to the Jira field value. If you selected the Map field value checkbox for a field in step 10, this step is necessary:

- For each CSV field value, enter the Jira field value.

- After assigning values to the fields, click Begin Import to begin the import procedure. Depending on the size of your data, this can take some time to finish:

13. You will receive a confirmation message letting you know how many issues have been imported once the import process is finished. Your CSV file should contain the same number of records as this number.

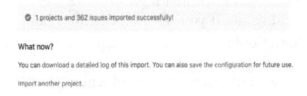

You can download the complete log file containing all the details for the import process by clicking the link labeled "Download a detailed log" on the final confirmation screen. If the import was unsuccessful, this is especially helpful.

Additionally, by selecting the link labeled "Save Configuration," you can create a text file containing all the mappings you created for this import. You can use this import file to avoid having to manually remap everything again if you need to run a similar import in the future. Check the box next to the option displayed in step 4 to use an existing configuration file.

We can see that Jira's project importer makes it simple to import data from other systems. To help Jira perform better, we will learn how to archive previous projects in the upcoming section.

Archiving projects and issues

Users may see Jira's performance deteriorating over time as they continue to utilize it. The Jira dashboard being loaded and looking for issues are two more obvious instances. Jira's performance is impacted by data size; the more projects, issues, and associated configurations (like custom fields) you have, the more data Jira will need to process and the slower it will be for your end users. The remedy to this issue is frequently the habit of archiving previous and unused projects.

Before Jira Data Center, you had to either export a project, delete it entirely, or hide the project and any issues by robbing users of their permissions. Both strategies are complicated and subject to mistakes.

A built-in archive capability in Jira Data Center now makes the procedure quick and reliable. You should take the following actions to archive a project:

1. Log into Jira with an administrator account.

2. Browse to Administration | Projects.

3. Select the Archive option for the project you wish to archive.

4. Confirm that you want to archive the project when prompted.

A project will no longer be listed for end users once archived. The archived project's issues won't come up in any searches. You can still access the problem if you have a direct link, but you cannot change it. All project-related information, including issues, will be deleted from Jira's search index when archiving a project. This will maintain a small index size and enhance overall performance.

Chapter 3: Using Jira for Agile Projects

Getting an overview of Scrum and Kanban

Scrum

The way Scrum prescribes the idea of iteration sets it apart from the waterfall paradigm. With Scrum, a project is broken down into several sprints or iterations, each lasting two to four weeks. A fully tested and possibly shippable product is produced at the end of each sprint.

The product owner and the team gather for a gathering known as a sprint-planning meeting at the start of each sprint. The focus of the upcoming sprint is selected during this meeting. In addition, top-priority tasks from the backlog are typically included, encompassing all unfinished work.

The team meets every day throughout each sprint to discuss progress, identify any potential issues or roadblocks, and make plans for how to overcome them. The purpose of these brief meetings is to ensure that everyone on the team is on the same page.

The team will gather to discuss the sprint results, look at what they did well, and discuss what they could have done better. The objective is to pinpoint areas that can be improved, which will inform subsequent sprints. Up till the project is finished, this process is repeated.

Kanban

Unlike Scrum, which operates in iterations, Kanban focuses more on the actual delivery of the product. It strongly emphasizes visualizing the delivery workflow from beginning to end, limits the number of work items in each workflow stage, and calculates lead times.

While using Kanban, it's crucial to visually track the progress of the work items, spot inefficiencies and bottlenecks, and then fix them. Work enters from one end and leaves from the other continuously to ensure that everything proceeds as quickly as feasible.

Running a project with Scrum in Jira

The first agile methodology we'll examine is Scrum. The active sprint agile board, which your team will use to track the progress of their current sprint, and the backlog, where you and your team will do the majority of your planning, make up the key components of a Scrum project in Jira.

Creating a Scrum project

Using the Scrum template is the first step in implementing Scrum in Jira. To do this, adhere to the following steps:

1. Choose to Create project from the Projects drop-down menu.

2. Click Next after selecting the Scrum software development template.

3. Click Next after agreeing to the options.

4. Click Submit after entering the new project's name and key.

The Scrum interface will open once the new Scrum project has been established.

The following are the primary sections of the Scrum interface:

- **Backlog:** All unforeseen problems are kept here. It can be compared to a to-do list. The development team and the product owner will collaborate to rank the items in the backlog, which will then be scheduled into sprints for completion.

- **Active sprints:** This view displays the active sprints as well as the issues that are related to them. The development team will utilize this to monitor their progress daily.

- **Reports:** You can generate several reports from this view to see how the project performs. These reports give you and your team a clear picture of how the project is doing and offer insightful criticism that you can apply to future sprint-planning meetings to make improvements.

Working with the backlog

Your project's backlog is a to-do list for all activities and incomplete features (typically expressed as stories). Therefore, the first stage is for the product owner and the team to collaborate on filling the backlog with stories and tasks that need to be accomplished because it may be empty when you first start. During this step, the team collaborates to transform customer and other stakeholder needs into executable stories and tasks, which functions more like a brainstorming session.

Prioritizing and estimating work

Once the backlog is full, the following step is to estimate and rank the issues so that you can plan and establish a timeline for their completion. Jira allows users to prioritize issues by moving them up and down the queue. For example, to increase the priority of an issue, you can move it up the backlog list. While it is frequently the product owner's responsibility to decide which features to deliver first, the team should also be involved in this decision-making process to ensure everyone knows the project's direction.

Your team's and your abilities to estimate, a critical part of Scrum, will greatly impact how successfully your sprints turn out. Because they think about estimation in terms of duration, such as whether story A will take five hours to complete or story B will take ten, people typically need to understand it. Even though this could first seem to be the truth, people often work longer than necessary to make the estimate seem realistic or provide huge estimates because they are still determining the task. It could become problematic as the project progresses since no one wants to be seen as the one who can't produce a reliable estimate or who is useless because they regularly go over budget.

One approach to avoid this pitfall is to estimate using a different method, such as narrative points, which is the default estimation strategy in Jira. The goal is to measure and estimate an issue's complexity rather than just relying on the required time to complete it. Because of this, if you start a sprint with 10 narrative points' worth of issues and cannot fix them all by the sprint's conclusion, it may indicate that you needed to be more ambitious and should have decreased your expectations. However, as the estimate is not based on the amount of time needed, it only indicates that you further divide the problems into more manageable portions because they might be too complicated. By doing so, you may more clearly identify the job at hand, divide it into smaller, easier-to-manage chunks, and stop people from constantly feeling like they are rushing the clock.

Nonetheless, there are times when it may take time to determine how intricate your story is. It usually serves as a red flag that you need to learn more about the story or that its focus must be more focused. The team needs to be aware of this and be bold in going back and asking more questions to fully understand the story's purpose before providing an estimate.

We can go forward now that we know how to estimate our challenges. The following steps can be taken to enter the estimate:

- Choose an issue to estimate from the waiting list.

- The Estimate section is where story points should be entered.

The estimate should be kept the same once the issue has been added to a sprint that is still in progress. Changing the estimate mid-sprint can lead to incorrect estimation during the spring planning period and potential future improvements.

Creating a new sprint

With the backlog populated and issues estimated, the next step is to create a sprint for the team to start working on. Note that you must have the Manage Sprints permission to create new sprints.

To create a new sprint, follow these steps:

1. Go to your project backlog.

2. Click on the Create sprint button.

3. Enter a name for the sprint.

4. Select the sprint duration and click the Create button. Generally speaking, you want to keep your sprint short. Between 1 and 2 weeks is usually a good length.

5. Add issues to the sprint by dragging and dropping issues prioritized by the team into the sprint box.

Once the team has decided on the scope, it's time to start the sprint:

1. Click on the Start sprint button.

2. Updating the sprint's duration is necessary. Click on the Start button to start your sprint.

Start New Sprint

This sprint contains **6 issues,** and **5 working days.** Learn more

Sprint Name:*	UI spring week 3
Goal:	Complete UI revamp.
Duration:	1 week ⌄
Start Date:	13/Mar/22 2:38 PM 🗓
End Date:	20/Mar/22 2:38 PM 🗓

Start Cancel

You can select the Custom option for the sprint's duration if you want to specify the end date of the sprint yourself instead of using the auto-calculated date.

Once the sprint has been started, you can go to the active sprints view, and the team can start working on the delivery.

If the Start sprint button is grayed out, you already have an active sprint running and do not have the parallel sprints option enabled or do not have the Manage Sprints permission.

Usually, you will only have one team working on the project at any given time. Still, if you have a big team and people can work on different project parts simultaneously, you must enable the Parallel Sprints option:

1. Log into Jira as an administrator.

2. Browse the Jira administration console.

3. Select the Applications tab and then Jira Software configuration.

4. Check the Parallel Sprints option to enable it.

Running a sprint

The agile board will change to the active sprint view after the team has ranked the issues and begun a sprint during the sprint-planning meeting. There will only ever be one active sprint for regular teams.

Each issue is represented as a card on the Scrum board, which comprises vertical columns that indicate the many states in which an issue may be and are mapped to the project's workflow. So, the default workflow in our case has three states: to do, in progress, and done. The project administrator will have the ability to alter this, as we will see later. When they work and finish their assignments, team members slide the issue card across the board into the appropriate columns.

In addition, the board can be divided into several horizontal rows known as swimlanes. They assist you in grouping related concerns and simplifying your board. In our illustration, we are classifying problems into swimlanes based on narratives. The project administrator can define swimlanes in whatever they want, just like columns.

The Scrum master and the product owner are responsible for ensuring that the team is not diverted or obstructed by any obstacles during a sprint to prevent scope creep. But, situations occasionally call for specific features or fixes to be added. In these circumstances, you can add new issues to the active sprint from the backlog view.

However, remember that this shouldn't become a regular occurrence because it is distracting and frequently indicates inadequate sprint planning or ineffective stakeholder communication. Jira will alert you if you attempt to add additional issues to an ongoing sprint because of this.

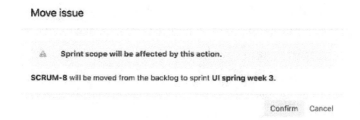

Move issue

⚠ Sprint scope will be affected by this action.

SCRUM-8 will be moved from the backlog to sprint UI **spring week 3**.

Confirm   Cancel

You must finish the sprint with the following actions:

1. Click Active sprints on the Scrum board.

2. Choose the link for the finished sprint.

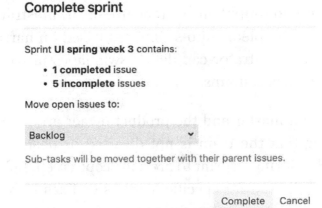

3. To end the sprint, click the Complete button.

Running a project with Kanban in Jira

After learning to manage projects using Scrum, it's time to examine Kanban, another agile methodology Jira supports. For teams new to agile, Kanban may be a simpler approach to learn and implement than Scrum. Kanban concentrates on execution and throughput measurement, unlike Scrum, which has a backlog and requires the team to prioritize and schedule their delivery in sprints.

A typical Jira Kanban board will differ from a Scrum board in the following ways:

- By default, there is no backlog view. Since there is no sprint-planning step in Kanban, your board serves as the backlog.

- The sprints are not running. The premise of Kanban is that work should flow continuously.

- Several kinds of reporting, tailored to Scrum and Kanban methodologies, have been created.

- Minimum and maximum restrictions are possible for columns.

- In cases where the limits are broken, columns will be highlighted. In the accompanying screenshot, we can see that constraint violations have been flagged in both the SELECTED FOR DEVELOPMENT and IN PROGRESS columns.

How to create a KanBan project

Creating a project using the Kanban template is the first step in using Kanban in Jira. Take these actions:

1. From the Projects drop-down menu, choose to Create project.

2. Click Next after selecting the Kanban software development template.

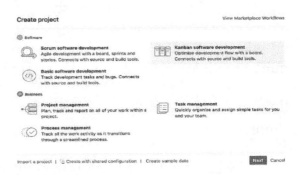

3. Click Next after agreeing to the options.

4. Click Submit after entering the new project's name and key.

After starting a Kanban project, you will be transported to the Kanban board view, which resembles the active sprint view of a Scrum board. Remember that using Kanban is similar to running a sprint that never ends or concludes after the entire project is finished. Therefore, the agile board assists you and your team in delivering.

How to use the KanBan board

As we just established, sprint planning is optional with Kanban. Thus, a backlog is unnecessary because everything is handled immediately on the Kanban board. The Kanban board is very easy to use; when a new problem is produced, it is immediately placed in the first column of the board, which is labeled BACKLOG (by default) and serves as your Kanban backlog. The team will then take issues from the BACKLOG column, assign them to the appropriate team members, and move them forward in the workflow. Issues may need to be reassigned to different users at different stages. For instance, when an issue enters testing from the development stage, it may need to be reassigned to a test engineer. You can set the board up to automatically remove finished issues after a certain amount of time as more and more issues are resolved, or you can do a release, which removes all issues with a DONE column from the board (still in the system). Regarding software development, where versions can be released, the option to use releases works better. The first option is good for teams using Kanban for general task management.

How to enable a KanBan backlog

For those of you from Scrum, not having a proper backlog may feel uncomfortable. As your project expands, displaying all new issues on the Kanban board in the BACKLOG column becomes too cumbersome. The good news is that Jira supports Kanplan, a hybrid Kanban/Scrum approach that enables you to build a backlog for Kanban.

Map the relevant status into the Kanban BACKLOG column to add a Scrum-style backlog to your Kanban project. Take these actions:

1. Explore the agile board for your project.

2. Choose Configure from the Board menu by clicking on it.

3. On the left menu panel, choose Columns. There is a column called BACKLOG by default.

4. The BACKLOG column should be removed.

5. Drag and drop the Backlog status that has been unmapped to the Kanban backlog on the left from the Unmapped Statuses column on the right.

Your backlog will now appear and function just like a Scrum project once a status has been mapped in the Kanban backlog column, and any newly produced issues will be added to the backlog because they are in the backlog workflow status.

Configuring agile boards

Jira's agile board may be significantly customized, and many of the choices use Jira's foundational elements, like workflows. Don't worry if you are unfamiliar with them. This section will examine these customization possibilities, starting with the board's column layouts.

How to configure columns

The default workflow built is relatively straightforward for both Scrum and Kanban, and the board's columns are mapped to the workflow utilized by the project. For instance, three statuses are available in the standard Scrum workflow: To Do, In progress, and Done. However, it needs to be revised, as projects also require testing and review as part of their development cycle. Follow these procedures to add new columns to your board:

1. Explore the agile board for your project.

2. Choose Configure from the Board menu by clicking on it.

3. On the left menu panel, choose Columns.

4. On the Add column button, click.

5. Choose a category and enter the new column's name. If your new column isn't replacing a To Do or Done column, it will often come under the In Progress category.

6. To position the new column correctly within your development workflow, drag & drop it into place.

7. If the column, such as Done, indicates that the problem has been resolved, choose the Set resolution checkbox. Doing this will automatically set the issue's resolution to Done.

How to add column constraints

Controlling the volume of work delivered is one of the essential components of Kanban, as we explained in the previous section.

While work restrictions are a Kanban idea, they are also occasionally utilized in Scrum projects. It enables you to employ Scrum for planning and Kanban for execution as part of the hybrid Scrumban approach.

Observe these procedures to configure column limitations for your agile board:

1. Explore the agile board for your project.

2. Choose Configure from the Board menu by clicking on it.

3. On the left menu panel, choose Columns.

4. In the Column Constraint option, choose how you want the constraint calculated. The Scrum board does not have any default constraints, whereas the Kanban board, by default, uses the Issue Count option.

5. Enter each column's minimum and maximum values to impose a constraint.

Once you've established the column constraints for your board, Jira will immediately notify you whenever one of the constraints is broken on your agile board.

How to set up swimlanes

As we previously observed, Jira's agile board allows you to organize related issues into horizontal rows known as swimlanes. Unlike columns assigned to workflow statuses, swimlanes can be defined based on any criterion, including your custom fields. To create swimlanes for your board, these steps should be followed:

1. Explore the agile board for your project.

2. Choose Configure from the Board menu by clicking on it.

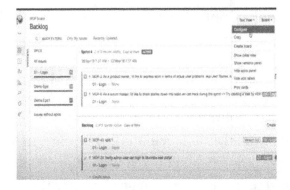

3. From the left navigation panel, choose Swimlanes.

4. In the Base Swimlanes on the field, specify how your swimlanes should be defined.

5. You must specify the query for each swimlane you want to add to the board if you select the Queries option.

Swimlanes are built using Jira Query Language (JQL) queries that you create. You must specify the JQL query for each swimlane that will return the issues you require for the swimlane. Problems will only be included in the first swim lane if they match multiple queries.

User tales will serve as the foundation for Swimlanes. The same swimlane will reveal subtasks that are a part of the same tale.

- **Assignees:** The swimlane will be determined by the assignee of each problem. The same swimlane will be used to group issues with the same assignee. This choice is made in the Scrum board in the Scrum section.

- **Epics:** Each issue of Swimlanes will be based on an epic. A swimlane will be created for each issue in the same epic.

- **Projects:** The basis of Swimlanes will be the project to which each problem belongs. The concerns from many projects can be included on an agile board, as we will see later in this chapter.

- **No Swimlanes:** As there won't be any swimlanes on the agile board, all issues will be arranged in a single row.

Defining quick filters

Your agile board will, by default, show every issue. All sprint-related issues will be included in Scrum, while any issues that have not yet been released will be included in Kanban. It might be rather distracting when you have many concerns and wish to concentrate on a few of them. Too many problems on the board can still be very noisy, even with swimlanes helping.

Jira can add several predefined filters to your board, which is a helpful feature. They enable you to filter out the concerns that don't concern you rapidly and only have those that appear on the board. However, it should be noted that this merely obscures the other issues from view; they remain on the board.

Just My Issues and Recently Updated are the two built-in fast filters already available in Jira. You can make your own by doing the following:

1. Explore the agile board for your project.

2. Choose Configure from the Board menu by clicking on it.

3. From the navigation panel on the left, choose Fast Filters.

4. The JQL query containing the filtered issues and the new filter's name must be entered.

Grooming your backlog

This will likely take up a significant portion of your daily routine if you use Scrum or Kanplan. It entails preventing high-priority things from being buried and ensuring they float to the top. In the case of Scrum, this is a continuous activity that becomes even more crucial as you and your team get closer to the beginning of a new sprint. Prioritizing tasks is equally important while using Kanplan so that your team can sustain throughput and avoid violating any limits due to bad planning.

Jira's backlog has several useful features that prevent backlog grooming from becoming tiresome. First, you just move the high-priority items up and the low-priority issues down in your backlog to prioritize the issues. Moving an issue from the bottom of a backlog with hundreds of issues to the top may seem easy initially, but as your backlog expands, it can become challenging. And remember that newly added issues automatically move to the bottom of the backlog. In this scenario, you can choose the Top of Backlog option from the Send to the menu by right-clicking the issue you want to relocate. The problem will rise to the top of the backlog as a result. You can also accomplish this with numerous issues by selecting them all with your keyboard's Shift or Ctrl key, then using the Send to menu or drag-and-drop to relocate them all.

Grooming the backlog is crucial to managing a Scrum or Kanban project successfully. A well-manicured backlog indicates that the issues are being examined, clarified, and prioritized. Teams will only be able to plan their sprint (in the case of Scrum) or what they should concentrate on with this.

Creating a new agile board for your project

Jira automatically creates an agile board for your project when you establish a new project using the Scrum and Kanban project template. You can make more boards for your project besides this default one.

For instance, if you developed a Scrum project and two teams are working on it, you may add a separate Scrum board for the second team so that they each have their agile boards and don't interfere with one another. Another illustration is that you can easily add a new Kanban board to the Scrum project if your second team needs to manage their portion of the project using Kanban. It will enable both teams to work on the same project using the agile methodology of their choice. These procedures should be followed to add a new agile board to your project:

1. Explore the agile board for your project.

2. Choose the Create board option by clicking the name of the current board in the top left corner.

3. To create a new board, choose the agile board you wish to use and follow the on-screen wizard.

Including multiple projects on your board

By default, when you create a new project, the agile board will only include issues from the current project. It is usually fine if your project is self-contained; however, there might be cases where you have multiple projects that are related or dependent on each other, and for you to get an overall picture, you need to have issues from all of those projects shown on a single agile board.

The good news is that Jira lets you do just this. One thing to understand here is that Jira uses a filter to define what issues will be included on the board. Filters are like saved search queries, and when a project is created, Jira automatically creates a filter that includes all of the issues from the current project. It's why the default agile board created with the project will always display its issues.

So, for you to include issues from other projects on the agile board, all you need to do is update the board by following these steps:

1. Browse your project's agile board.

2. Click on the Board menu and select the Configure option.

3. Select the General option from the left navigation panel.

4. Click on the Edit Filter Query link for the Saved Filter option if you want to update the filter currently being used by the board.

Chapter 4: Working with Issues

I ssues is one of the fundamental building blocks in Jira – almost all of Jira's features and concepts revolve around issues.

Understanding issues

In Jira, an issue often refers to a discrete task that users will complete. Depending on Jira's use, an issue might reflect different items and concepts in the actual world. An issue, for instance, could be a bug or a narrative in a software development project or an IT service project. On the other hand, it might be an incident or a support request.

Although an issue may represent many different things, all issues in Jira share the following crucial characteristics:

- A project must contain an issue.

- It needs to have a type, also called an issue type, that describes what the problem stands for.

- A summary is necessary. The summary functions as a one-line summary of the topic at hand.

- It needs to be in status. An issue's status reflects where it is in the workflow at any given time.

A task in a business project, a software development project narrative, or a service desk project request are a few examples of work units that can be completed by a user represented by issues in Jira. These all represent various problem categories.

Jira issue summary

To represent a piece of work or a task that needs to be finished, an issue in Jira can be anything in the real world. First, we'll examine the issue presented in Jira's business and software project user interfaces.

The following is a description of its sections:

- Project/issue key: This identifies the project to which the issue pertains. The specific identifier of the present issue is the issue key. A breadcrumb is provided in this section to make navigation simple.

- Issue summary: Here is a brief explanation of the problem.

- Issue export options: These are several alternatives for exporting the issue. There are three choices: XML, Word, and Printable.

- Issue operations include actions like Edit, Assign, and Add Comments that users can take on an issue. They are detailed in this chapter's following sections.

- Workflow transitions: These are the options for workflow transitions. Chapter 7, Workflow and Business Process will address workflows.

- Issue details/fields: This includes issue Type and Priority. This section also consists of a display of custom fields. In Issue fields: Fields of the user type, such as Assignee and Reporter, are covered in this section. In Chapter 5, Field Management, fields are covered.

- Date fields: Date-type fields, including Created and Updated, are specifically covered in this section.

- Attachments: All of the issue's attachments are listed here.

- Sub-task list: Issues can be divided into more manageable subtasks. Subtasks for an issue will be listed here if there are any.

- Comments: This displays all comments that the current user can see.

- Work log: This contains a list of every time-tracking entry one of your users has made about the issue. For more information, refer to the Tracking time section.

- History: Records all alterations to this problem, including the values used before and after the alteration.

- Activity: This is comparable to History. However, it is presented in a more streamlined manner. Moreover, it can produce an RSS feed for the content.

Issues will be displayed as cards on the agile board, which offers a more condensed description of issues when utilizing Jira with Scrum or Kanban.

Working with issues

Jira is focused on issues, as we've already seen. In the following sections, we'll look at what you, as a user, can do with concerns. First, you must have certain rights to perform each of these tasks.

How to create an issue

There are various fields you must fill out when creating a new issue. For example, the issue's summary and kind are required, whereas other fields, including the description, are optional.

You can make a new issue in Jira through several different methods. You can choose between the following possibilities:

- Choose "Create" from the top banner by clicking on it.

- On your keyboard, hit C. The Create Problem dialog box will appear.

There are a lot of fields, as you can see, and the necessary ones will have a red asterisk next to their names.

The administrator predetermines the Create Issue dialog fields. However, users can personalize and create their own Create Issue screens by hiding the optional fields by taking the following actions:

1. At the top-right corner, select Configure Fields.

2. Choose Custom Fields from the menu.

3. Uncheck all the fields you want to hide and tick the boxes next to the fields you want to display.

You can only add new issues if you hide any mandatory fields. You're just concealing or displaying these fields for your benefit.

How to assign issues to users

The user typically assigned to an issue will begin working on it as soon as it is created. The user may then reassign the problem to QA personnel for further investigation.

An issue may need to be assigned to another person in various situations, such as when the existing assignee is unavailable or when issues are produced without a designated assignee. Another illustration is the assignment of concerns to various individuals at various phases of the workflow. Jira enables users to reassign issues after they have been created because of this.

To assign a problem, perform the actions below:

1. Go to the problem you want to assign.

2. On the Issue menu bar, click the Assign button or press A on your keyboard (you can also use the inline edit feature here). The Assign dialog will appear as a result.

3. Choose the new assignee for the problem, and you can optionally add a remark to provide the new assignee with some information.

4. On the Assign button, click.

Once the new user has been assigned to this problem, the Assignee value will be changed to reflect this. Also, a notification email informing the new assignee of the assignment will be sent to them Alternatively, you can unassign a problem by only choosing the Unassigned option. Unassigned issues do not have an assignee and must be shown on everyone's list of open issues.

How to edit an issue

You can modify an issue in Jira in one of two ways:

- The first, more conventional method involves hitting the Edit button or pressing the E key on your keyboard. It will open the Edit Issue dialog box and display all the editable fields for the current issue. It enables you to modify numerous fields at once.

- Inline editing is the second choice. Using this method, you can view the problem immediately and edit the desired field without waiting for the edit dialog to load. Instead, place your mouse over the value of the field you want to update, select the Edit (pencil) icon, and begin editing to edit a field inline.

The screen for the edit issue procedure determines the fields you can edit. Not all fields can be modified; some are read-only, and some specialized fields might not appear while examining the issue.

How to move an issue between projects

An issue is linked to the project it was made in once created. Yet, you can transfer the problem from one project to another. Although it may seem like a relatively straightforward process, there are a lot of processes and factors to consider:

- If the new project does not have the existing problem type, you must first choose a new issue type for the issue.

- If the target project or issue type employs a different procedure, you must map a status for the issue.

- It would help if you chose the values for any required fields in the new project but not in the existing one.

Jira includes a wizard that can assist you in addressing all of these issues.

To start moving a problem, follow these steps:

1. Find the problem you want to transfer by browsing.

2. On the More menu, select the Move option. The Move Problem wizard will then appear as a result.

The Move Issue wizard consists of four steps:

1. The first step is choosing the project to which you want to transfer the issue. It would help if you also chose the new issue type. You can frequently continue and use the same issue type if it's present in the new project.

2. The second phase lets you map the present problem to the new project's process. The wizard will skip this step if the target project already contains the issue's status.

3. The third phase displays all required fields and fields in the new project but not the current one.

4. The fourth and final phase displays an overview of the modifications made after the issue is transferred from the source project to the destination project. It is your final opportunity to verify the accuracy of all the data. You can return to step one and start over if you need

corrections. By clicking on Move, you can confirm the move if you're satisfied with the modifications.

Once it has been relocated, the issue will receive a new issue key based on the new project. Jira will immediately reroute you if you try to access the issue using the old issue key.

How to share issues with other users

Instead of manually copying and pasting the issue's URL into an email, you may utilize Jira's built-in share tool to send issues to other users via email. To share an issue, navigate to it, click the share symbol, or hit S on your keyboard. Next, click the Share button after choosing the users you wish to share the issue with.

How to delete an issue

Issues can be removed from Jira. Although it is usually preferable to close and label the issue as a duplicate, you might need to erase issues that were accidentally created or if the issue is redundant.

In Jira, deleting an issue is irreversible. Jira entirely removes the problem from the system, unlike other systems that may store deleted records in a trash bin that you can retrieve later. The deleted issue can only be recovered by restoring Jira from an earlier backup.

To delete an issue, follow these instructions:

1. Find the problem you want to remove by browsing.

2. Choose Delete from the More menu by clicking on it. The Delete Problem dialog box will appear.

Delete Issue: SCRUM-10

Please confirm that you wish to delete this issue.

Deleting an issue removes it permanently from Jira, including all of its comments and attachments.

If you have completed the issue, it should usually be resolved or closed - not deleted.

Note: issue's 2 sub-tasks will be deleted.

Delete   Cancel

3. Click the Remove button to delete the problem from Jira permanently.

It should be noted that deleting an issue permanently deletes it along with all of its associated information, such as attachments and comments.

Issue linking

You can design unique links for issues in Jira. It allows you to elaborate on the problem. For example, you can link to other Jira issues or arbitrary web resources, such as a web page, using one of two different links.

How to linking issues with other issues

Issues frequently have some connection to one another. For example, issue C could be a copy of Issue D, or Issue A could be obstructing Issue B. Maintaining track of all these relationships using this method is challenging, even if you add descriptions to the issue or delete one if it is duplicate to convey this information. Thankfully, Jira's normal issue link functionality offers a simple fix for this.

Using the standard issue link, you can link an issue with one or more other issues in the same Jira instance. It implies that you can connect two issues from various projects (if you have access to both projects). The target issues to link to must be known to link issues in this manner, which is extremely easy. The steps listed below can be used to link issues:

1. Visit the view Issue page if you want to build a link for it.

2. Links can be chosen from the More menu. The dialog box for link issues will appear as a result.

3. Choose Jira Issue from the left panel's menu.

4. From the This issue drop-down menu, choose the issue linking type.

5. Choose the issues you want to connect to. You can find the issues you're looking for using the search function.

6. Click on the Link button.

Your issues will appear in the Issue Links area on the See Issue page once you have linked them. In addition, the target issue's key, description, priority, and status will be shown in Jira.

How to link issues with remote contents

Using the normal Jira issue link, you can link numerous issues to the same Jira instance. Jira also enables you to link issues to resources, such as online web pages.

The difference between using remote issue links and ordinary issue links is that instead of choosing another problem, the URL address of the intended resource is supplied. The steps listed below can be used to set this up:

1. Open the link issue dialog box.

2. From the left panel, choose the Web Link option.

3. Provide the destination resource's URL address. Jira will automatically look for the right icon for the resource and load it.

4. In the Link Text field, enter the link's name. The link will be shown with the name you choose here upon viewing the issue.

5. Click on the Link button.

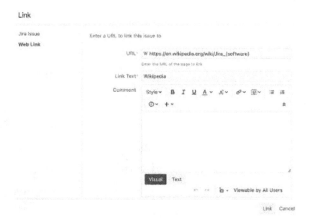

Jira enables you to provide issues with extra context by using issue linking.

Tracking time

It makes sense for users to track the time they have spent working on an issue because they frequently represent a single unit of work that may be worked on. Jira can assist you in monitoring the status of an issue if you give the expected work needed to resolve it.

The Time Tracking panel on the right-hand side of Jira shows the time tracking data for a given problem.

The following details are included in the Time Tracking panel:

- Estimated: This shows the initial estimated effort needed to resolve the issue and the projected time needed for a developer to repair a bug.

- Time left: This is the amount of time that has to pass for the problem to be resolved. Jira determines it automatically based on the initial estimate and all user-logged time. However, the user logging work on the problem can also override this value.

- Logged: This shows how much time has been spent on the problem overall.

Specifying original estimates

The original estimates represent the projected time needed to finish the task reflected by the issue. A blue bar is displayed next to the Time Tracking section.

It would help if you made sure that the Time Tracking field is added to the issues create and/or edit screens for you to specify an original estimate value.

When establishing or amending an issue, enter a value in the Original Estimate field to specify the initial estimate value.

Logging work

You may record your time working on an issue in Jira by logging your work. As long as you have permission, you can log work on any of the issues. To track work done on a problem, take these steps:

1. Click on the issue you want to log work for.

2. Out of the More menu, choose Log Work.

3. Choose the duration you want to record. To specify the week, day, hour, and minute use the notation w, d, h, and m, respectively.

4. Choose the day you want to record your work.

5. Optionally, decide how to modify the remaining estimate.

6. Provide a summary of the work you have completed.

7. You can choose who can see the work log entries.

8. Click on the log button

You have the choice of how the remaining estimated value will be impacted when you log work on an issue. By default, this figure will be determined automatically by deducting the logged amount from the initial estimate. The remaining estimate can be set to a specific value or reduced by a different amount than the documented work. Still, you can also choose from other possibilities that are offered.

Issues and comments

Users of Jira can post comments on issues. You can add comments when assigning an issue to a different user. It is a beneficial tool enabling group collaboration so that users can work on the same problem and exchange knowledge. For instance, by adding a comment to the issue, the support staff (issue assignee) may ask the business user (issue reporter) for additional explanation. Automatic email alerts will be sent to the issue's reporter, assignee, and any other users viewing the issue when used with Jira's built-in notification system.

All users logged in by default can comment on issues they have access. Follow these steps to add a comment to an issue:

1. Find the article you want to comment on by browsing.

2. Press M on your keyboard or the Comment button to leave a comment.

3. Comment by entering it in the text box. You can limit who can see your comment and preview it.

4. The remark may be added by clicking the Add button.

Issue type and sub-tasks

As we already saw, issues in Jira can stand in for various things, from project management milestones to software development tasks. One issue type can be distinguished from another by the issue type.

Each problem has a kind (hence the name issue type), so the Issue type column identifies that type. In addition, it informs you of the nature of the problem and facilitates the choice of numerous other details, such as the fields that will be shown for this problem.

Although out-of-the-box issues are excellent for software development projects, they may only sometimes satisfy other people's demands. Jira allows you to define your issue categories and assign them to projects because it is impossible to design a system that can meet everyone's expectations. For instance, you could develop a special problem type called a ticket for a support desk project. Users can enter tickets rather than bugs into the system if you create this unique problem type and add it to the Help Desk project.

The administration page for managing issue kinds is called Manage Issue Types. To reach this page, take the following actions:

1. Become a Jira administrator by logging in.

2. Go to the Jira management console.

3. Choose the Problem types option after selecting the Issues tab. It will direct you to the page for issue types.

Creating issue types

The creation of custom problems kinds has a wide range of applications. When you want your issues to reflect something other than the standard issue kinds, that is the most frequent use case. Applying multiple configurations for the problems in a particular project is another frequent use case. For example, you want specific issues in a project to have a distinct set of fields. In that case, you can create a new issue type and apply the configuration scheme to that issue type exclusively because most Jira configuration schemes are based on project and issue types. Follow these procedures to establish a new problem type:

1. Access the Issue Types page.

2. To add a new issue type, click the button.

3. For the new issue type, enter its name and description.

4. Choose between a regular issue type and a sub-task issue type for the new problem type.

5. To add a new issue type, click Add.

The new problem type will be given a default icon after creation. You must first select a new image as the issue type's icon by clicking on the Modify link for the issue type.

Deleting issue types

You must remember that an issue type can already be in use, which means that issues have already been produced with that issue type while deleting it. So, you will need to choose a new issue type for those issues when you delete one. Jira handles this for you, which is terrific news. Jira notifies us of the 10 issues now of the Bug type when we delete the Bug issue type.

Delete Issue Type: Bug

Note: This issue type cannot be deleted - there are currently 10 matching issues with no suitable alternative issue types (only issues you have permission to see will be displayed, which may be different from the total count shown on this page).

In order for an issue type to be deleted, it needs to be associated with one workflow, field configuration and field screen scheme across all projects. If this is not the case, Jira can not provide a list of valid replacement issue types.

Cancel

Using sub-tasks

Only one person (the assignee) may work on one issue at a time in Jira. With this system, an issue is always treated as a single piece of labor that can be attributed to a single person. But in the real world, we frequently encounter circumstances that call for numerous individuals to work on the same problem. It can be due to a bad task breakdown or just the nature of the current task. Whatever the cause, Jira offers a solution to this issue through sub-tasks.

A sub-task is just another issue type, as we saw earlier when talking about issue kinds. The only distinction is that there must always be a parent issue for a sub-task.

You can have one or more subtasks for each issue, each of which can be assigned and monitored independently. Other sub-tasks are not permitted in sub-tasks. Jira only permits subtasks at one level.

As sub-tasks are associated with issues, you must first go to the issue to create a new sub-task by following these steps:

1. Go to the problem you want to add a subtask to.

2. Choose to Create sub-task under More in the menu.

You will see the well-known New Issue dialog box, but you'll notice that, unlike when you create an issue, you are not given the option of choosing which project to create the sub-task in. It is so that Jira can assess the value of the project based on the parent issue. You'll also observe that you are limited to choosing issue categories that are subtasks.

Except for these differences, a typical issue can be created like a sub-task. You may quickly create numerous sub-tasks and modify the fields in the dialog box by choosing the Create another option.

After creation, the sub-task will be added to the parent issue's Sub-Tasks section. You can view the status of each of the issue's related subtasks. A green check mark will appear next to a sub-task once finished.

Sub-Tasks			+ ...
1. ✓ Prepare contract document		DONE	Patrick Li
2. Send contract to legal for review		IN PROGRESS	Alana Grant
3. Deliver contract to client for signature		TO DO	Jennifer Evans

Issue type schemes

Projects may use issue-type schemes, which are collections or templates of different problem categories. Jira has a default issue-type scheme for all projects without specific issue-type schemes. When you create a new project based on your chosen template, a new issue-type scheme is generated for you. Issue types will also be pre-populated in the new scheme using the template. We have several problem-type schemes, and Jira will identify the projects utilizing them.

Adding issue type to an issue-m type scheme

To build a fresh problem-type scheme, Take these steps:

1. Get to the administration console by clicking.

2. Choose the Issue type schemes option after selecting the Problems tab. You'll be taken to the Problem type schemes page as a result.

3. Select the Edit link for the issue type scheme to add issue types.

4. Drag and drop the issue types from the Available Issue Types list into the Issue Types for the Current Scheme list to include them in the scheme.

5. Choose a number for the default issue type. Choosing a preset issue type for a new scheme is completely voluntary and can only be done after at least one issue type has been chosen.

6. Choose "Save" from the menu.

Once your issue type scheme has been established and configured, you can associate it with one or more projects by clicking the Associate button and choosing the projects you want to use the scheme on.

Chapter 5: Field Management

Issues are collections of fields, while projects are groups of issues. Data is gathered by fields and can then be displayed to users. Jira has various fields, from straightforward text fields where you can enter alphanumeric text to more intricate fields with pickers for selecting dates and individuals.

Understanding field searchers

Collecting data is only half of an information system. Jira is no different in that users will need to be able to find the information later on, typically through searching. Jira's fields are in charge of storing and displaying data, but their related searchers are in charge of handling searches.

A custom field searcher controls how the field's data will be indexed, which affects how you can search the field's data. A text custom field, for instance, will index its data as raw text so that you may perform a fuzzy search on the text beginning with a specific character. On the other hand, a select list custom field will index its data differently, allowing you to perform searches on a specific option value or a list of option values. You can only search a field's data if a searcher has been applied; otherwise, the data will not be indexed.

Jira comes with searchers for every field, allowing you to find issues based on their summary or assignee without having to do any further settings. In addition, some custom fields from third-party add-ons may have multiple searchers available. By modifying the custom field, you can modify the default searcher.

Custom field context

Jira has universal system fields like Summary and Issue Type. It indicates that all issues and projects have access to these fields. Contrarily, custom fields, sometimes called context, can be used with particular projects and problem kinds.

Projects and problem kinds are combined to form a custom field context. Jira will examine the project and issue type of the current problem to see if there is a specific context that matches the combination when you are dealing with an issue. Jira will show the custom field with unique parameters, such as selection options if one is discovered. The custom field won't be shown if no context is detected.

Customization and speed are the two key justifications for using custom field contexts.

For example, end users have alternatives when using custom field types with choose lists and radio buttons. You can modify the available alternatives for various projects, issue types, or situations. It eliminates duplication by allowing you to utilize the same custom field for numerous projects.

Performance is the second advantage of employing custom field context. When Jira displays an issue, it will only need to show custom fields with contexts for the problem if you limit your custom fields to specified project and issue categories. The response time will be quicker the fewer custom fields Jira needs to show.

Jira does not have a custom field for the issue if no context matching the project and issue type combination can be discovered. In the section on adding custom field contexts, we will examine how to set custom field contexts. You must now keep in mind that you must ensure that a custom field has the appropriate context setting before adding it.

Managing custom fields

Jira uses custom fields universally, so you must have the Jira Administrator global access to administrative tasks like creation and configuration.

Jira keeps track of all custom fields in one place for simple maintenance. To access the Manage custom field page, follow these steps:

1. Become a Jira administrator user and log in.

2. Go to the Jira management console.

3. Then click the Custom fields button under the Problems tab.

How to add a custom field

Jira has a wizard to guide you through the multi-step process of adding a new custom field. When adding a new custom field, there are two required stages and one optional.

First, you must choose the kind of custom field. As the field type cannot be modified once selected, it is crucial to get it right. You must consider the field's intended usage, the kind of data you wish to keep, and how you will search the data when selecting the field type.

If you are adding a Select List custom field type, you must first name the custom field type once you have made your choice. Choosing which screens to add the field to is the last optional step.

We'll take you through it step by step:

1. Go to the website for custom fields.

2. Select the option for Add Custom Field. You can choose the custom field type at step 1 of the procedure by doing this.

3. Select the type of custom field you'd like to create from the drop-down menu, and then click Next. You can then define the name and available options for the custom field in step 2 of the procedure. Keep in mind that you can't switch the field type after it's been created, regardless of what sort of field was originally chosen:

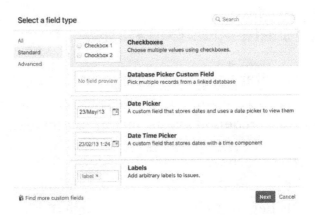

4. Fill out the Name and Description fields with numbers. You must also add the select choices for any selection-based custom fields you create, such as select lists (you can edit this list later):

5. Choose the new custom field's setting. A custom field's scope should be narrowed to include only the kinds of issues and projects for which it will be useful. After the custom field has been made, the setting can be altered.

6. Select "Make" from the menu. Selecting this option will take you to the last stage of the procedure, where you can choose which page the field will appear on. This stage is not necessary because Jira already has the custom field added. The area does not need to be added to a screen.

7. Choose the screens, then select Update. The accompanying screenshot demonstrates the new field's incorporation into two different views:

How to editing/delete a custom field

Whenever after creating a custom field, you can alter its specifics. You may have already seen that each custom field has two options: Configure and Modify. Making the distinction between the two may take a lot of work. In the following sections, we will review settings relating to the custom field context specified by configure. The custom field's name, Description, and search templates are among the parameters that are specified in the edit form and are applicable across Jira:

1. Go to the page for custom fields.

2. From the list of custom fields, click the cog icon next to the custom field you want to edit, then choose the Edit option.

3. The custom field's name or search template can be changed.

4. To make the changes effective, click the Update button.

Existing custom fields may also be deleted:

- Go to the page for custom fields.

- Choose the Delete option by clicking the tools symbol next to the custom field you want to delete.

- To remove the custom field, click the Delete button.

Once a custom field is destroyed, it cannot be recovered, and the data it contains cannot be retrieved or searched. In addition, Jira assigns unique IDs to each custom field, so if you attempt to create another custom field with the same type and name, it will not inherit the data from the prior custom field.

Configuring a custom field

You must go to the Configure Custom Field page to configure a custom field:

1. Go to the page for custom fields.

2. Click on the cog icon next to the custom field you want to configure in the list of custom fields and choose the Customize option. Doing so will take you to the Configure Custom Field page.

How to add custom field contexts

It's easy to create a new custom field context. The only thing left to do is choose the project and issue type combination to establish the context:

1. To establish a new context for a custom field, navigate to the Configure Custom Field page.

2. Choose the link for "Add new context." You will then be directed to the context page for the Add configuration scheme.

3. In the Configuration scheme label field, type a name for the new custom field context.

4. Under the Pick appropriate problem types section, choose the issue categories for the new context.

5. Under the Pick relevant context section, choose projects for the new context.

6. To create a new custom field context, click the Add button.

How to configure select options

The custom field must be chosen first, followed by the context to which the choices will be applied, to configure choose options:

1. Go to the page for custom fields.

2. Click on the Configure option to configure the select options for a custom field.

3. Click the Modify Options link to apply the settings to a custom field context.

The Add button will add the value once you enter the option values in the Add New Custom Field Options section. The options will be included in the system in the order that they are entered. You can manually reorder option values by clicking and dragging them or click Sort options alphabetically to let Jira handle it for you.

When you're done configuring the select choices, click the Done button.

How to set default values

In the same way that selection options are specified, default options are likewise set for each unique custom field context:

1. Go to the page for custom fields.

2. Select options for the custom field you want to configure and click the Configure option.

3. Click the Modify Default Value link to apply the default values to the custom field context.

4. Set the custom field's default value.

5. To set the default value, click the Set Default button.

Optimizing custom fields

Jira includes a custom field optimizer to aid in that. Follow these steps to launch the optimizer:

1. Go to the page for custom fields.

2. At the top right corner, select the Optimize link.

3. Click the Scan button to do a new scan of your custom fields.

After the scan is finished, Jira will provide you with a report on several ways you may optimize your custom field configurations to assist in boosting the speed of Jira as a whole.

Field configuration

Fields are used in Jira to collect and present data. Field configuration determines the behaviors that can be applied to fields. For example, you can set up the following behaviors for each field in Jira:

- **Field description:** When an issue is modified, a description text for the field is displayed beneath it. Field settings allow you to have distinct description text for various projects and issue categories.

- **Visibility:** A field's visibility controls whether it should be shown or hidden.

- **Required:** This indicates whether a field will be needed to have a value when an issue is created or amended or whether it will be optional. It will eliminate the None option from the list when used with select, checkbox, or radio button custom fields.

- **Rendering:** It describes how the field will appear when you modify it and how the content will be displayed. For instance, a text-based field might include two text editors: the plain text-based default editor and the rich-text editor, which lets you style your content in various ways.

How to add a field configuration

It is easy to create new field configurations. All you have to do is give the new configuration a name and a succinct description:

1. Visit the page titled See Field Configurations.

2. The Add Field Configuration button should be clicked.

3. Enter a name and description for the new field configuration.

4. To create a field configuration, click the Add button.

How to manage field configurations

To access field configuration options, perform these steps:

- Visit the page titled See Field Configurations.

- For the field setting you to want to configure, click the Configure link. You'll then be sent to the View Field Settings page.

Field descriptions

While giving your fields, meaningful names can assist users in understanding what they are used for, adding a brief description will add additional context and meaning. Field descriptions are shown beneath the fields when creating or editing an issue. Do the following to add a description for a field:

- For the field configuration you want to utilize, navigate to the See Field Configuration page.

- To add a description to a field, click the Edit link.

- Then click Update after adding a description.

Required fields

By default, when you add a new field to Jira—such as a custom field—it is optional, so users are not required to enter a value. However, afterward, you may modify the configuration to make those fields necessary:

1. For the field configuration you want to utilize, navigate to the See Field Configuration page.

2. For the field where you want to make a requirement, click the REQUIRED/OPTIONAL link.

Field visibility

In Jira, most fields can be made invisible to users. Users cannot see a field when it is set to Hidden on any screen, including those for creating, updating, and viewing. To reveal or conceal a field, take these actions:

- For the field configuration you want to utilize, navigate to the See Field Configuration page.

- For each field you want to show or hide, click the Show/Hide link.

Field rendering

When a field is viewed or modified, renderers determine how it will be shown. You can select the renderer for some systems and custom fields with several renderers. For example, for text-based fields like Description, you can choose between the basic text renderer and the more sophisticated wiki-style renderer, enabling you to add more customization using wiki markup.

Jira includes four distinct renderers by default:

The default text renderer for fields that only accept text. Plain text is produced for the contents. The renderer automatically converts any text that resolves a Jira issue key into an HTML link.

- **Wiki-style renderer:** This improved renderer is used for fields that contain text. It enables you to embellish your text content with wiki markup.

- **Renderer for select lists:** This is the default renderer for fields that use selections. It is displayed like a typical choose list in HTML.

- **Autocomplete renderer:** This improved renderer helps users as they begin typing in the fields by offering an autocomplete feature. It is designed for selection-based fields.

Field configuration scheme

Jira decides when to use each of the numerous field configurations through the field configuration scheme. First, field configurations are mapped to issue kinds using a field configuration scheme. Then, this scheme may be connected to one or more projects.

It enables you to simultaneously apply numerous field configurations tied to different problem kinds to a project. Then, depending on the nature of the problem, the project can decide which field configuration to use. For instance, you can have various field settings for tasks and problems within the same project.

Because each scheme may be reused and linked to many projects, grouping configurations into schemes allows you to reuse existing configurations without doing additional work.

How to add a field configuration scheme

You only need to provide the scheme's name and an optional description to create a new field configuration scheme:

1. Go to the page titled See Field Configuration Schemes.

2. The Add Field Configuration Scheme button should be clicked.

3. To create a new field configuration scheme, enter a name and a description.

4. To build the scheme, select Add from the menu.

How to configure a field configuration scheme

You can add a mapping between field configurations and issue kinds once you've put up a new field configuration scheme. One issue type can only be mapped to one field configuration for each field configuration scheme. However, each field configuration can be mapped to many issue types.

How to associate a field configuration scheme with a project

The steps below can be used to link a field configuration scheme to a project:

- Go to the administrative page for the desired project.

- In the left panel, select the Fields option.

- From the Actions menu, choose to Use a different scheme.

- Click on the Associate button after selecting a new field configuration scheme.

Chapter 6: Screen Management

Fields collect data from users, and you have seen how to create custom fields from a wide range of field types to address your different requirements. Indeed, data collection is at the center of any information system, but that is only half of the story. It is just as important to have your fields organized so that users feel safe, and the general flow of fields needs to be logically structured and grouped into sections. It is where screens come in.

Understanding Jira and screens

It would help if you first comprehended what screens are and how Jira uses them before you can begin working with them. For example, Jira fields like checkboxes and blank areas on a typical paper-based form and displays resemble the form documents. Therefore, Jira fields must be put on screens for users to see after they are generated.

Screens are typically connected to actions like creating, viewing, and editing issues. Screen schemes specify this relationship. It enables you to use various screens for various operations. When applied to projects, screen schemes will be mapped to issue types due to their association with issue-type screen schemes. As a result, every issue in a project might have its own set of displays. A screen will only be utilized directly in connection with a process transition. Jira workflows outline the numerous states that an issue may take. An issue might go from open to close, for instance. Jira allows you to display a screen as part of the activity if you transition an issue from one state to another.

Working with screens

Jira is quite adaptable when customizing displays, unlike many other software systems that provide users little flexibility over how screens are presented. You can design your screens and choose which fields appear on them and in what order. Moreover, you can choose which screens should be shown when doing issue activities. You can design and build unique screens in Jira for the following tasks:

- Opening the New Issue dialog box to create an issue

- Updating an issue while it is still being edited

- Seeing a problem after a person has created a problem and is viewing it

- Advancing a problem through a workflow

How to add a new screen

The default displays and the screens automatically generated for your projects can meet the most fundamental needs, but you will quickly outgrow them and need to make improvements. For instance, you can accomplish this by setting up different screens for creating and updating issues if you wish to keep some fields, like a priority, or read-only, so they cannot be modified after issue creation. Another illustration uses various

Create and Modify panels for various issues, such as Task and Bug. In these circumstances, you must follow the procedures below to create your screens in Jira:

1. Browse to view the screens page.

2. Choose "Add screen" from the menu. The Add screen dialog box will then appear as a result.

3. Give the new screen a descriptive name that makes sense. It's a good idea to give your screen a name that reflects what it's for, such as HD: Bug Creation Screen, to signal that it's for adding new bug issues for project HD.

4. To create the screen, click the Add button.

Your new screen is now empty and devoid of any fields. With Jira, fields are ordered and shown in a single column, from top to bottom. The fields that can be added and the order in which they can be placed are completely within your control.

How to add a field to a screen

A screen is not very useful when it is first made. You must first add fields to the screens before you can show the users with items:

1. For the screen, if you want to add fields, too, click the Customize link.

2. By typing the field's name into the Field name dropdown list, you can choose the fields you want to add. When you type, Jira will automatically match the field. Check to see if the field you are looking for is already on the screen or a separate tab if you can't find it.

How to delete a field from a screen

Follow these steps to remove a field from the screen:

1. For the screen from which you want to remove fields, click the Customize link.

2. Click the X (remove) button while your mouse is over the field you want to remove.

If you delete it from a screen, existing issues will not lose their value for a field. The values will be seen once you add the field back.

How to add a tab to a screen

Any screen in Jira can have tabs added to it. All screens have a default tab named Field Tab, which houses all the fields. To organize and better manage your screen display, you can add new tabs to a screen:

1. Browse the view screens page

2. To add a new tab, select the Customize link for the screen on which you want to do it.

3. Click the plus sign (+) above the field list to name the tab.

4. To create the tab, click the Add button.

The linear arrangement of the tabs is from left to right. A new tab is added to the conclusion of the list when it is added to the screen. As seen in the accompanying screenshot, you can reorder the tabs in the list by dragging them left and right:

How to edit/delete a tab

Just like screens, you can maintain existing tabs by editing their names and/or removing them from the screen. Perform the following steps to edit a tab's name:

1. Browse to the View Screens page.

2. Click on the Configure link for the screen with the tab you wish to edit.

3. Select the tab by clicking on it.

4. Click on the edit icon and enter a new name for the tab.

5. Click on the Save button to apply the change.

Follow these instructions to delete a tab:

1. Visit the website for View Screens.

2. On the screen where the tab you want to change is located, click the Configure icon.

3. Clicking on the link will select it.

4. Select the erase button. Jira will ask you to confirm your decision before listing every field that is currently visible and deleting the tab.

5. The tab will be removed from the screen when you click the Delete option.